Z

A Pilgrim's Song

A PILGRIM'S SONG

GEOFFREY DEARMER

*Selected Poems to mark the Poet's
100th Birthday*

Foreword by Jon Stallworthy

Compiled by Laurence Cotterell

JOHN MURRAY

First published in 1993
by John Murray (Publishers) Ltd.,
50 Albemarle Street, London W1X 4BD

Reprinted 1993, 1997

A catalogue record for this book is available from the British Library

ISBN 0–7195–5242–7

Typeset in 10½/12 Bembo by Wearset, Boldon, Tyne & Wear
Printed in Great Britain by
Butler & Tanner, Frome and London

TO CHRISTOPHER

Killed, Suvla Bay, October 6th, 1915

At Suvla when a sickening curse of sound
Came hurtling from the shrapnel-shaken skies,
Without a word you shuddered to the ground
And with a gesture hid your darkening eyes.
You are not blind to-day –
But were we blind before you went away?

Forgive us then, if, faltering, we fail
To speak in terms articulate of you;
Now Death's celestial journeymen unveil
Your naked soul – the soul we hardly knew.
O beauty scarce unfurled,
Your blood shall help to purify the world.

Awakened now, no longer we believe
Knight-errantry a myth of long ago.
Let us not shame your happiness and grieve;
All close we feel you live and move, we know
Your life shall ever be
Close to our lives enshrined eternally.

FOREWORD

Geoffrey Dearmer was born in 1893, the same year as Wilfred Owen, and brought up in the same religious faith and the same literary tradition. He went to the Great War before Owen; survived what his poem 'Mudros, After the Evacuation' calls the 'needless horror of the Dardanelles', a horror for him compounded by the death of a much-loved brother; and went on to experience the horrors of the Western Front. These, too, he survived – unlike his famous contemporary. Both young poets identified themselves with Keats, under sentence of death the celebrant of life. Dearmer, in the first of his two poems about this admired exemplar, 'Keats, Before Action', calls to mind the 'Ode on a Grecian Urn' as someone else in the same situation might whisper a prayer:

> A little moment more – O, let me hear
> (The thunder rolls above, and star-shells fall)
> Those melodies unheard re-echo clear
> Before the shuddering moment closes all.

Edmund Blunden would summon up the same lines on the same Front in 'Vlamertinghe: Passing the Château, July 1917', but whereas he uses the impending sacrifice of Keats's heifer to comment bitterly on the generals' impending sacrifice of himself and his friends, Dearmer's poem ends not with indignation but with celebration of a 'truth' that most soldiers 'Before Action' would deny:

> Enough – enough – let lightning whip me bare
> And leave me naked in the howling air
> My body broken here, and here, and here.

vi

Beauty is truth, truth beauty – that is all,
The very all in all.

The poet who could so view the prospect of his own
dismemberment had written earlier, in his dedicatory poem
to his brother Christopher, 'Killed, Suvla Bay, October 6th,
1915': 'Your blood shall help to purify the world'. In the
same year, Siegfried Sassoon addressed *his* brother – also
killed at Gallipoli – in similarly positive terms. He and
Owen, however, would later come to a more desolate
vision, articulated in a language that rejected the old pieties,
the old poetic diction, as Dearmer did not. Happily for him,
his trust in God survived the horrors, and he was sustained –
even more than Edmund Blunden – by the ministering
beauty of a natural world that never ceases to bind the
wounds that man unnaturally inflicts:

> Turn where you will. Look, there a signboard shows
> The lair of guns; already round the sign
> White trumpeting convolvuli entwine
> Their clinging arms, across the placard blows
> A quiet-breathing rose.

One does not have to share Geoffrey Dearmer's beliefs to
respect them and to recognize that he speaks for many less
articulate victims of the Western Front. No doubt his
seemingly unshaken vision of this world and the next helped
to sustain him and bring him safely home to make a fresh
start, like that recommended in the sestet of one of his
sonnets:

> O love, my love, time shall your body wither,
> But you have put like Browning in your breast
> Power of your spirit's youth, an eagle's feather,
> Golden in service and in friendship blessed,
> Come, let us start freshly again together,
> And let's remember to forget the rest.

His post-war poems are, almost without exception,
poems of celebration – poems that 'remember to forget the

rest' – but in one of the most recent, the old soldier speaks, with characteristic wit, as an old soldier:

LORD, when I stand in Thy celestial court
And render thee a poet's last report;
From my worn, working body, dearly prized,
Discharged, or, at the best, demobilised;
Curse me if so thou must, thou art divine,
And say that little verse is worse than mine;
Blue-pencil all, but give me not, I pray,
Upon that (O, I hope long-distant) day
My poems back complete, corrected, clean –
Lord, show me not how good they should have been!

For once, it is safe to predict the verdict of the court, as it is an honour and a pleasure to salute one of the oldest of our old soldiers and the oldest of our old poets.

Jon Stallworthy,
Wolfson College, Oxford
November 1992

CONTENTS

Foreword   vi

Introduction   xi

THE DARDANELLES   1
    From 'W' Beach   2
    The Turkish Trench Dog   3
    The Sentinel   4
    A Prayer   6
    The Dead Turk   7
    Mudros, After the Evacuation   8

B.E.F.   9
    Missing   10
    The Storm Night (Trench Poem I)   14
    Resurrection (Trench Poem II)   14
    Gommecourt   15
    Tell Me, Stranger   20
    Spring in the Trenches   21
    On the Road   22
    Keats, Before Action   24
    The Somme   25
    Somme Flower Talk   28
    To the Uttermost Farthing   29
    A Trench Incident   32
    The French Mother to her Unborn Child 33
    Envoi   34

POTPOURRI *or* WHAT YOU WILL   35
From The Death of Pan   36
    'We Poets of the Proud Old Lineage'   43

The Shadow   44
Everychild   45
Child of the Flowing Tide   47
Eight Sonnets: I   48
                 II   48
                 III   49
                 IV   49
                 V   50
                 VI   50
                 VII   51
                 VIII   51
Keats   53
Reaction   54
The Strolling Singer   55
Ambition   60
A Blessing   61
Farewell to Romany   63
Dear Love the Past   64
Come, Let's not Brief . . .   65
Unseen   66
Bon Voyage   67
Song from the Selsea Pageant, 1965   68

OTHER CREATURES SEEN LIGHTHEARTEDLY   69
  The Brontosaurus   70
  Blue Whale   71
  Birds   72
  The Snake   73
  The Giraffe   74
  The Duck-Billed Platypus   76

CONCLUSIONS   77
  Hands   78
  A Prayer, II   79
  A Pilgrim's Song   80

Acknowledgements   81

INTRODUCTION

Geoffrey Dearmer is properly described as 'poet' – a proud
title so often claimed prematurely and arrogantly self-
assumed. Those discriminating publishers, William Heine-
mann in 1918 and John Murray in 1923, would not other-
wise have issued his works under their renowned imprints.
The innate modesty and self-deprecation which have until
now prevented publication of a truly representative selec-
tion of his poems, also led to Geoffrey Dearmer's careless-
ness about keeping reviews of his early volumes. However,
I have managed to unearth just one notice of each, and these
alone give him accolade.

Robert McBride, reviewing the 1918 *Poems* in the *New
York Times* wrote, 'This is the first book of a young English
soldier-poet whose work has aroused the admiration of
English critics everywhere. Mr Dearmer is, *par excellence*, a
poet of the war; not that he glorifies bloodshed in any way,
but because in each of the poems the vision of battle holds
the foreground. His work is characterised by an extreme
simplicity of form that seems almost austere, but there is no
lack of feeling in it or in the author. Even in the most
unassuming of his verses, such as *The Turkish Trench Dog*,
there is dignity that approaches grandeur.'

John Harvey, reviewing the 1923 collection, *The Day's
Delight*, in *Fortnightly Review* said that 'This little collection
of poems is the essence of Mr. Dearmer's continuous work
during the last five years. His verse is familiar to literary
lovers of flowers and animals. Certain of his songs have
been set to music, and his long poem, *The Death of Pan*,
extracts from which are included in this volume, caused
quite a sensation on its original appearance . . .'

Geoffrey Dearmer's ranking in relation to the well-known poets of the Great War of 1914–18 is a matter for the assessment of recognised critics more perceptive and authoritative than I. Whatever that assessment may be, I have no doubt about the impact he has had, and will have, on the feelings of innumerable people of widely differing outlook and background. His distinctive note is one of hope and uplift despite exposure to the horrors not only of the trenches, but also the hell of Gallipoli (where his adored younger brother was killed).

The poet's father, Percy Dearmer, was a London vicar who eventually became a Canon of Westminster. He was well known as author of *The Parson's Handbook*, and acknowledged as a leading authority on hymns, being responsible for the *English Hymnal*. Geoffrey's mother, Mabel, was a celebrated *Yellow Book* illustrator, also writing children's books, novels and plays. She died of enteric fever in 1915 while serving with an ambulance unit in Serbia. Her moving *Letters from a Field Hospital* were published posthumously.

During the inter-war years, Geoffrey Dearmer wrote and published a continuous flow of verse, plays and novels, though he took little interest in keeping copies of his works or press notices. Among other things, he was responsible, as a member of the Incorporated Stage Society, for putting on the first showing of R.C. Sherriff's *Journey's End*. When I went to see him recently (nudging his century as he is) he was still amused by remembrance of his stint as Examiner of Plays for the Lord Chamberlain in the days of theatre censorship. A less censorious man it would be difficult to meet in a long day's march! For many years thereafter he worked for the BBC, notably as a highly imaginative and creative director of Children's Hour, that immensely popular and influential radio feature of a pre-television era.

In making this selection I have had access to the Heinemann and Murray collections, and also to the booklet of Geoffrey Dearmer's own favourites, which he put together and published privately for his friends. Other poems of his, many of them appearing over the years in various periodicals, may surface from one quarter or another. Conversely, some thirty or so of the poems in the three collections mentioned are not included in this book. Several of these exclusions are quite delightful facetiae – passing comments that would not harmonize with the rest in such a selection – or have been omitted for other reasons.

As regards a title, my first proposal for this was *A Taste of Dearmer*. Indeed, if the appearance of this collection should evoke curiosity concerning his other verses, there might be a case for a further selection.

In the event, the publishers and I agreed to observe the author's wishes and give the book the same title as his own booklet, *A Pilgrim's Song*, since his life has been a many-faceted journey of exploration – mental, physical and spiritual – in differing milieux, in war and peace or so-called peace. Yet, paradoxically enough, the particular piece of his work with that title, 'A Pilgrim's Song' is not truly poetry. It is a hymn, a pious, simple expression of faith and hope by a good and gentle man, who has never allowed the horrors of war at the sharp end, or the rigours and disillusionments of so-called peace, to embitter him or lead to the iconoclastic, sometimes nihilistic cynicism besetting so many minds today in the mistaken belief that it is realism.

Although I cannot remember the text precisely, I think Lord Dunsany once wrote that most men walk with heads bowed, and see the mud swirling round their feet, and find realism only in the mud. Yet a few walk with their heads up, and see the stars, finding reality in the stars. There is the difference, perhaps, between realism and reality, for the stars are just as real as mud. Since emerging from childhood, and for the better part of a century, Geoffrey Dearmer has looked to the stars, even when the bloodied mud of the battlefields was swirling round his boots.

Although there are Acknowledgements at the end of the book in which I proffer due and sincere thanks to the donors, publishers, trustees and others whose generosity and altruism have helped to bring this collection into being,

I must, here and now, express special and intense gratitude to Dame Catherine Cookson, without whose staggering contribution of more than half the total sum needed for production and publishing, the whole project would have been abandoned. With as many solicitations from promoters of good causes as any other public figure, this is not merely a generous gesture in honour of a fellow author. It is munificence!

Laurence Cotterell
St Paul's Cray, Kent
November 1992

THE DARDANELLES

FROM 'W' BEACH

The Isle of Imbros, set in turquoise blue,
  Lies to the westward; on the eastern side
The purple hills of Asia fade from view,
  And rolling battleships at anchor ride.

White flocks of cloud float by, the sunset glows,
  And dipping gulls fleck a slow-waking sea,
Where dim steel-shadowed forms with foaming bows
  Wind up the Narrows towards Gallipoli.

No colour breaks this tongue of barren land
  Save where a group of huddled tents gleams white;
Before me ugly shapes like spectres stand,
  And wooden crosses cleave the waning light.

Celestial gardeners speed the hurrying day
  And sow the plains of night with silver grain;
So shall this transient havoc fade away
  And the proud cape be beautiful again.

Laden with figs and olives, or a freight
  Of purple grapes, tanned singing men shall row,
Chanting wild songs of how Eternal Fate
  Withstood that fierce invasion long ago.

THE TURKISH TRENCH DOG

Night held me as I crawled and scrambled near
The Turkish lines. Above, the mocking stars
Silvered the curving parapet, and clear
Cloud-latticed beams o'erflecked the land with bars;
I, crouching, lay between
Tense-listening armies peering through the night,
Twin giants bound by tentacles unseen.
Here in dim-shadowed light
I saw him, as a sudden movement turned
His eyes towards me, glowing eyes that burned
A moment ere his snuffling muzzle found
My trail; and then as serpents mesmerise
He chained me with those unrelenting eyes,
That muscle-sliding rhythm, knit and bound
In spare-limbed symmetry, those perfect jaws
And soft-approaching pitter-patter paws.
Nearer and nearer like a wolf he crept –
That moment had my swift revolver leapt –
But terror seized me, terror born of shame
Brought flooding revelation. For he came
As one who offers comradeship deserved,
An open ally of the human race,
And sniffing at my prostrate form unnerved
He licked my face!

THE SENTINEL

An Episode at the Evacuation of Gallipoli

He stood enveloped in the darkening mist
High on the cape that proudly kept her tryst
Above the narrow portal. All the day
White shell-flung water-spouts had scattered spray
Round Helles, warden of the Eastern seas;
And still the boom of Asian batteries
Rumbled around the cape. The sentinel
Spied from his high cliff-towered citadel
The leaping flash of guns; but ere the roar
Sprang from its den on the dim Asian shore,
He blew a trumpet. Then, like burrowing moles,
Dim forms below dashed headlong to their holes,
The while that hurtling iron crossed the sea,
And fifteen seconds seemed eternity.
                Below we lay
Crushed in a lighter; and the towering spray
That lately blurred the clear star-laden sea
Subsided in the vast tranquillity.
Now, chafing like taut-muscled charioteers
With every sense on tiptoe, we strained ears
For whispers, or the catch of indrawn breath.
Still not the word to cut adrift the rope
That moored us to a wharf of floating piers:
And thus alternately in fear and hope
Swung the grim pendulum of life and death.

Then suddenly the sound
Of that loud warning rang the cape around.
We knew a gun had flashed, we knew the roar
That instant rumbled from the Asian shore;
And we lie fettered to a raft! . . . The shell

Climbs its high trajectory . . . Well,
What of it? Fifteen seconds less or more
One – two – three – four – five – six – seven
(Steady, man,
It's only Asiatic Ann) . . .
How slow the moments trickle – eight – nine – ten
(They're wonderful, these men).
Am I a coward? I can count no more;
Hold Thou my hands, O God.

The sea, upheaved in anger, rocked and swirled;
Niagara seemed pelting from the stars
In tumult that epitomised a world
Roused by the battling impotence of wars.
We heard a whispered order to escape,
And casting loose, incredulously free,
Unscathed, exulting in the amber light,
We left behind the immemorial cape.

But still above the indomitable sea
From his high cliff a sentry watched the night.

A PRAYER

Lord, keep him near to me:
Revive his image, let my darkening sight
Renew his life by death intensified
(His beating life so pitifully tried)
That we may face the night
And shade the agony.

We pray in barren stress
Where stricken men await the shrill alarm
And nightly watch, in silent order set,
The beckoning stars enshrine the parapet.
Lord, keep his soul from harm
And grant him happiness.

When all the world is free,
And, cleansed and purified by floods of pain
We turn, and see the light in human eyes;
When the last echo of War's thunder dies;
Lord, let us pause again
In silent memory.

Gallipoli, October 1915

THE DEAD TURK

Dead, dead, and dumbly chill. He seemed to lie
Carved from the earth, in beauty without stain.
And suddenly
Day turned to night, and I beheld again
A still Centurion with eyes ablaze:
And Calvary re-echoed with his cry –
His cry of stark amaze.

MUDROS, AFTER THE EVACUATION

I laughed to see the gulls that dipped to cling
To the torn edge of surf and blowing spray,
Where some gaunt battleship, a rolling king,
Still dreams of phantom battles in the bay.
I saw a cloud, a full-blown cotton flower
Drift vaguely like a wandering butterfly,
I laughed to think it bore no pregnant shower
Of blinding shrapnel scattered from the sky.
Life bore new hope. An army's great release
From a closed cage walled in by fire and sea,
From the hushed pause and swooping plunge of shells,
Sped in a night. Here children in strange peace,
Seek solitude to dull the tragedy
And needless horror of the Dardanelles.

Mudros, January 1916

B.E.F.

MISSING

They told me nothing more: I bow my head
And squander life, between the quick and dead
Irresolute. Yet I again could be
Mistress of life, Queen of my destiny,
If I but knew – But now Remembrance plays
My being back through spring and summer days
We passed together; and I see him still
Swinging to meet me down the tardy hill.
That day the birds were new-inspired; a breeze
Bestirred, as if in wonderment, the trees;
The very clouds paused in their breathless race,
And shadows played upon his open face;
And I remember how his laughing eyes
Shone deep as pools in sea-blue ecstasies.
The meadow grasses rustled in the heat;
I even heard the silence of his feet
Down the slow hill – And now the dawning birth
Of beauty woke my senses to the earth
Unveiled in radiance. The sweeping skies –
Unseen unless reflected in his eyes –
Marshalled cloud companies with new delight;
Just for us two the spangled dome of night
Swung out the journeying moon.
                                        But still I hold
Burnt in my memory in beaten gold
Days when the Spring stirred in each waking bush
A blue-flecked jay or tawny-feathered thrush,
And drowsy Winter, startled unawares
By arc-winged partridges or listening hares,
Fled guiltily. We heard the magpies call –
Those dominoes at Nature's carnival –
And once a kingfisher, a lovely gleam

Snatched from a rainbow, darted to a stream.
The snowdrops bowed their heads for us to see,
Shy peeping buds of hooded chastity;
And stalwart cowslips raised sun-glinted eyes
To those who stooped to pluck their sanctities.
Grass-nestled crocuses that scorn the wind
Speared upward proudly and besought mankind
To step with care. Near by, we searched a glade
Where violets brood in sweetness, half afraid
To wake their petals. On we roamed, and soon
The flower that shares her secret with the moon
In pale gold fellowship peeped out, among
A host of truculent daffodils that flung
Their trumpets down the wind.
                              Each breathless day
Broke to fulfil its promise, till the May
Had fledged her clustered blooms and swung her pride
In bowing sweetness to the countryside.
Beauty was born again. But now the sound
Of heavy Autumn patters to the ground,
And loud discordant booms of thunder roll
Where that enchanted owner of my soul
Lies dead, or dying, or is living still:
At last the fibres of my struggling will
Falter exhausted, and my cowering brain
Cries out in anguish like a child in pain.

If he is dead, then I abide to prove
That brief fulfilment may be perfect love.
How should I grieve? His life inspired in me
A joy that shall outlive eternity,
Wrought out, complete, unsnared by time and age
My jewelled past my priceless heritage.

11

Shall misery usurp my realm of years
And leave me drowning in self-pitying tears,
A derelict in my own whirlpool swirled –
Me – whom Love crowned an empress of the world?
                              But sometimes ere the light
Glimmers dawn-pearled to splash the feet of night,
Ere red, sun-gilded riot floods the sky,
A whisper, swelling to a ringing cry,
Tells me he's living still. No lash could sting
Like this persistent voice re-echoing
That mocks me as I stumble to my feet.
O, shall I find him wandering in the street?
But every beckoning corner drags me past
Strangers, new faces, each one like the last
Dull, cold, inscrutable. At times I caught
The look – the walk – the gesture that I sought;
And once with throbbing veins I found those eyes
That shone like pools in sea-blue ecstasies,
But looked beyond me – cold expressionless
In vacant wonder at my helplessness.
                              Then, haunted by that stare,
Beaten, I knew the bedrock of despair.
O, Thou who poised the world, are all my tears
Too light, too pitiful to reach Thine ears?
Locksmith of happiness, aloof, apart,
Am I too impotent to touch Thine heart?
Tell me he's dead or dying; say he stands
Seeking for guidance the warm touch of hands,
Doomed in an instant to eternal night,
With only mind and memory for sight –
For I could cheer him.
                              But Lord quench this drought,
The unfathomable immensity of doubt,
Tell me he's maimed or crippled, torn or blind,

Staring through eyes that show his wandering mind –
Tell me he's rotting in a place abhorred –
Not this, not this, O Lord!

TWO TRENCH POEMS

I

THE STORM NIGHT

Peal after peal of splitting thunder rolls
(Still roar the howling guns, and star-shells rise)
We perish, drowned in anger-blasted holes,
Give ear, O Lord! Our very manhood cries,
Shell-fodder yea – but spare our human souls
From fury-shaken skies!

II

RESURRECTION

Five million men are dead. How can the worth
Of all the world redeem such waste as this?
And yet the spring is clamorous of birth,
And whispering in winter's chrysalis
Glad tidings to each clod, each particle of earth.
So the year's Easter triumphs. Shall we then
Mourn for the dead unduly, and forget
The resurrection in the hearts of men?
Even the poppy on the parapet
Shall blossom as before when Summer blows again.

GOMMECOURT

I

The wind, which heralded the blackening night,
Swirled in grey mists the sulphur-laden smoke.
From sleep, in sparkling instancy of light,
Crouched batteries like grumbling tigers woke
And stretched their iron symmetry; they hurled
Skyward with roar and boom each pregnant shell
Rumbling on tracks unseen. Such tyrants reign
The sullen masters of a mangled world,
Grim-mothered in a womb of furnaced hell,
Wrought, forged, and hammered for the work of pain.

For six long days the common slayers played,
Till, fitfully, there boomed a heavier king,
Who, couched in leaves and branches deftly laid,
And hid in dappled colour of the spring,
Vaunted tornadoes. Far from that covered lair,
Like hidden snares the sinuous trenches lay
'Mid fields where nodding poppies show their pride.
The tall star-pointed streamers leap and flare,
And turn the night's immensity to day;
Or rockets whistle in their upward ride.

II

The moment comes when thrice-embittered fire
Proclaims the prelude to the great attack.
In ruined heaps, torn saps and tangled wire
And battered parapets loom gaunt and black:
The flashes fade, the steady rattle dies,
A breathless hush brings forth a troubled day,

And men of sinew, knit to charge and stand,
Rise up. But he of words and blinded eyes
Applauds the puppets of his ghastly play,
With easy rhetoric and ready hand.

Unlike those men who waited for the word,
Clean soldiers from a country of the sea;
These were no thong-lashed band or goaded herd
Tricked by the easy speech of tyranny.
All the long week they fought encircling Fate,
While chaos clutched the throat and shuddered past,
As phantoms haunt a child, and softly creep
Round cots, so Death stood sentry at the Gate
And beckoned waiting terror, till at last
He vanished at the hurrying touch of sleep.

The beauty of the Earth seemed doubly sweet
With the stored sacraments the Summer yields –
Grass-sunken kine, and softly-hissing wheat,
Blue-misted flax, and drowsy poppy fields.
But with the vanished day Remembrance came
Vivid with dreams, and sweet with magic song,
Soft haunting echoes of a distant sea
As from another world. A belt of flame
Held the swift past, and made each moment long
With the tense horror of mortality.

That easy lordling of the Universe
Who plotted days that stain the path of time,
For him was happy memory a curse,
And Man a scapegoat for a royal crime.
In lagging moments dearly sacrificed
Men sweated blood before eternity:
In cheerful agony, with jest and mirth,
They shared the bitter solitude of Christ

16

In a new Garden of Gethsemane,
Gethsemane walled in by crested earth.

They won the greater battle, when each soul
Lay naked to the needless wreck of Mars;
Yet, splendid in perfection, faced the goal
Beyond the sweeping army of the stars.
Necessity foretold that they must die
Mangled and helpless, crippled, maimed and blind,
And cursed with all the sacrilege of war –
To force a nation to retract a lie,
To prove the unchartered honour of Mankind,
To show how strong the silent passions are.

III

The daylight broke and brought the awaited cheer,
And suddenly the land is live with men.
In steady waves the infantry surge near;
The fire, a sweeping curtain, lifts again.
A battle-plane with humming engines swerves,
Gleams like a whirring dragon-fly, and dips,
Plunging cloud-shadowed in a breathless fall
To climb undaunted in far-reaching curves.
And, swaying in the clouds like anchored ships,
Swing grim balloons with eyes that fathom all.

But as the broad-winged battle-planes outsoared
The shell-rocked skies, blue fields of cotton flowers,
When bombs like bolts of thunder leapt and roared,
And mighty moments faded into hours,
The curtain fire redoubled yet again:
The grey defence reversed their swift defeat
And rallied strongly; whilst the attacking waves,
Snared in a trench and severed from the main,

17

Were driven fighting in a forced retreat
Across the land that gaped with shell-turned graves.

IV

The troubled day sped on in weariness
Till Night drugged Carnage in a drunken swoon.
Jet-black with spangling stars athwart her dress
And pale in the shafted amber of the moon,
She moved triumphant as a young-eyed queen
In silent dignity: her shadowed face
Scarce veiled by gossamer clouds, that scurrying ran
Breathless in speed the high star-lanes between.
She passed unheeding 'neath the dome of space,
And scorned the petty tragedy of Man.

And one looked upward, and in wonder saw
The vast star-soldiered army of the sky.
Unheard, the needless blasphemy of War
Shrank at that primal splendour sweeping by.
The moon's gold-shadowed craters bathed the ground –
(Pale queen, she hunted in her pathless rise
Lithe blackened raiders that bomb-laden creep)
But now the earth-walled comfort wrapped him round,
And soon in lulled forgetfulness he lies
Where soldiers clasping arms like children sleep.

Sleep held him as a mother holds her child:
Sleep, the soft calm that levels hopes and fears,
Now stilled his brain and scarfed his eyelids wild,
And sped the transient misery of tears,
Until the dawn's sure prophets cleft the night
With opal shafts, and streamers tinged with flame,
Swift merging riot of the turbaned East.
Through rustling gesture loomed the advancing light;

Through fitful eddying winds, grey vanguards came
Rising in billowy mountains silver-fleeced.

And with the dawn came action, and again
The spiteful interplay of static war:
Dogged, with grim persistence Blood and Pain
Rose venomous to greet the Morning Star.
But others watched that lonely sentinel
Chase fleeting fellow-stars before the day;
Fresh men heard tides of thunder ebb and flow.
– Stumbling in sleep, scarce heeding shot or shell,
The men who fought at Gommecourt filed away:
The poppies nodded as they passed below.

They left the barren wilderness behind,
And Gommecourt gnarled and dauntless, till they came
To fields where trees unshattered took the wind,
Which tossed the crimson poppy heads to flame.
But one stood musing at a waking thought
That spurred his blood and dimmed his searching eyes –
The primal thought that stirs the seed to birth.
Here where the battling nations clashed and fought
The common grass still breathed of Paradise
And Love with silent lips was Lord of Earth.

B.E.F., 1916

TELL ME, STRANGER

Tell me, Stranger, is it true
   There is magic happening,
Are *all* the dappled fields of Kew
   Bowing to their Lord the Spring?

Are the bluebells chaste and mute
   Dancing in each dale and hollow
Dew-sprinkled, with a glad salute
   To omnipotent Apollo?

Tell me, do the feathered creatures
   Flutter as in days of yore,
What are the 'distinctive features'
   Of the Swallow's Flying Corps?

Here there is no magic, Stranger,
   Save within our merry souls –
For some wanton god in anger
   Punches earth with gaping holes.

Yet the stifled land is showing
   Here and there a touch of grace,
And the marshalled clouds are blowing
   Through the aerodromes of space.

Hate is strong, but Love is stronger,
   And the world shall wake to birth
When the touch of man no longer
   Stays the touch of God from Earth.

Tell me, Stranger, is it true
   There is magic happening,
Are *all* the dappled fields of Kew
   Bowing to their Lord the Spring?

B.E.F., April 1917

SPRING IN THE TRENCHES

The racing clouds have borne her message down
And blown a thrilling rumour, from the far
Heart-centres of each crowded port and town,
And up the flowing arteries of War.
Life, life, green tales of corn in sprouting blades,
Of swallows crowding with sea-sprinkled wings
And ash-buds amber-gummed round close-furled green.
High blossom mantling murmurous orchard glades
In air a-tingle April-sweet and keen –
Ah, we have heard of wondrous happenings.

For now the magic carnivals begin
The lilac broods in honeyed secrecy,
And dappled lawns are changed: a Harlequin
Has brushed the tangled carpet silently.
We know how white narcissus fills the lake
With dancing shadows; how in open blue
A chestnut builds her clustered pyramids,
And down below anemones awake;
Long-hushed the violets open the wide their lids
And all the dreamed-of fantasy comes true.

Glad tidings thrill the re-awakened earth
By daffodils and blue-bells heralded;
Spring with her van imperial comes forth
To herald Summer proudly canopied
Beneath the bowing leaves. Persistent Spring
Bestirs the seed enshrined in Winter's store;
And even round the parapet a breath
Of far-flung prophecy is clamouring:
'Behold new life within the tomb of death
'Importunate and vivid as before.'

ON THE ROAD

We halted, with the urgent Spring behind
Our straining teams, where all the land was black,
And huddled woods lay beaten, starkly blind:
Their mangled branches loomed athwart the track
Grotesque and terrible. Yet near the way,
A river, scatheless as the open sea,
Flowed like a breathing hope that cannot die
In desolation. Now, at setting day,
Moored water lilies, pale as argent sky,
Cling to the twilight fading silently.

Such is the tale of memory, ere night
Had deepened, and our weary convoy slept
Beside the way. Slow-rising points of light
Twinkled amid the spangled netting swept
Across the ebon desert; and a gleam
Pierced the cloud-woven pillows of the moon.
Now slumber freed me from the iron cage
That bound the snarling war; and, in a dream,
The panorama of a dawning age
Unrolled, a world slow-waking from a swoon.

Before my gaze a teeming city loomed
Gay with the bustling clamour of the street –
The very town an easy world had doomed
And cast in ashes at the trampling feet
Of mortal gods. Street, corner, square and place,
Seemed woken from a long and squalid trance –
I saw a nation growing like a flower;
A nation true and loyal to a race
That forged an army of clean-soldiered power
Wrought by the common chivalry of France.

Here was no arrogance of martial pride,
The fireside boast that sows the fatal seed,
For happiness had come from those who died
Stark of delusion and the deadly creed
Of false romance. I saw a world reborn –
The very battlefield was robed again
In lines of chequered land, and bordered round
With stretching roads and rills. The poppied corn
Held rubies set in gold, and far beyond
Lay a surf-ravelled sea and swarded plain.

I marvelled, till oblivion shadowed all,
Blurred in the dawning light of every day.
It was so true, I scarcely heard the call
To feed and water and to move away.
We stretched our limbs, and packed each heavy load;
Moved on, and left the weary night behind,
Through torn and withered trees that stared aghast;
Yet, through the veil that shrouded all the road
I saw new radiance in the land we passed,
And heard a sudden murmur in the wind.

B.E.F., 1917

KEATS, BEFORE ACTION

A little moment more – O, let me hear
(The thunder rolls above, and star-shells fall)
Those melodies unheard re-echo clear
Before the shuddering moment closes all.
They come – they come – they answer to my call,
That Grecian throng of graven ecstasies,
Hyperion aglow in blazing skies,
And Cortez with the wonder in his eyes.
In battle-wreaths of smoke they rise, and fall
Beyond – beyond recall.

Now all is silent, still, and magic-keen
(Yet thunder rolls above and star-shells fall)
And slowly pacing, rides a faery queen
Wild eyed and singing to a knight in thrall.
Enough – enough – let lightning whip me bare
And leave me naked in the howling air
My body broken here, and here, and here.
Beauty is truth, truth beauty – that is all,
The very all in all.

THE SOMME

From Amiens to Abbeville
My swollen waters race,
And silver-veined by many a rill
Green hamlets thrive apace.
From Amiens to Abbeville
I labour at the listless mill,
And tempt the nodding daffodil
To blur my open face.
But south of Amiens I flow
Past dumb Peronne and Brie,
The peopled land I used to know
Now all belongs to me.
Yet phantom armies come and go,
And shadows hurry to and fro;
Again my seething battles grow
In murdered Picardy.

Behold the mother of a soil forlorn;
I suckled towns, and fed the forest land,
Behold my shattered villages and mourn
How should I understand?
Why are those huts o'erpatched like dappled kine,
What are those weary men in blue and brown,
And humming craft that search my sinuous line;
Why should my name re-echo with renown
Past every phantom town?
But still my lily-breasted waters shine,
And still I chant my shadowy ripples down.

From peace through war my waters flow,
To peace again at sea,
The peopled land I used to know
Now all belongs to me.

Though battling armies come and go,
I toil and spin, I reap and sow,
And poppy-mantled meadows blow
In murdered Picardy.

My eddies bear the clinging scent of lime
To sweeten clouds of plume-tossed meadowsweet;
My meadow grasses nestle with the thyme
And flowering rushes tower in the heat.
Low-brushing swifts and swallows splashed with white
O'er flash my laden mirrors slow and deep
That bear swift-merging canopies of sleep.
Until the growing light
Has chased marauding owls, and butterflies,
Born of blue-woven skies,
Flutter away like hare-bells spurred to flight.
But who are these? The powdered butterfly
Outshines that air leviathan that swings
In rigid curves adown the barren sky,
With cloudy satellites about her wings.
And I have seen
Dark horsemen ride with spears of tapered steel;
And bellowing guns beneath the far balloons.
And once a ponderous slug bedecked in green
Crept, in the waning moon's
Still-darkening gloom, and at her giant heel
White-gleaming, ran a train of hooded cars . . .

I triumph, triumph, search my sinuous line
Amid the snarling impotence of wars.
Turn where you will. Look, there a signboard shows
The lair of guns; already round the sign
White trumpeting convolvuli entwine
Their clinging arms, across the placard blows
A quiet-breathing rose.

And still my lily-breasted waters shine
And loud my chanting grows:

> From peace through war my waters flow
> To peace again at sea,
> The peopled land I used to know
> Now all belongs to me.
> Though battling armies come and go
> I toil and spin, I reap and sow,
> And poppy-mantled meadows blow
> In murdered Picardy.

SOMME FLOWER TALK

Said the Cornflower to the Pimpernel,
   'O sudden scarlet eyes,
You never bloomed till ploughing shell
   Laid bare earth's sanctities!'

Then upward cried the Pimpernel:
   'Blue head in deeper blue,
'Tis strange this former waste of Hell
   Is Paradise anew.

'But who is Lord of Paradise
   And Commandant; and who
Commands sky-faring butterflies
   All camouflaged in blue?

'Are dandelion parachutes
   His messages, and do
Those armoured beetles clamber roots
   With news from Army Q?

'Above each water-lily ship
   The feathered red caps pipe,
Because the pear has earned a pip,
   The tiger-moth a stripe.

'The gorse artillery has eyes
   We never knew before.
And lady bees can organise
   The Honey Service Corps.

'Field-marshals rule the war behind
   The guns, but Summer shields
Here in the clash of human kind
   Her marshal of the fields.'

TO THE UTTERMOST FARTHING

'He too! He too!' The veteran paused, the sound
Of a light paper fluttering to the ground
Rustled the twilight peace. 'He – too – is – dead – '
His wife, scarce faltering from the words she read,
Stared at the glowing sun, the while her eyes
Shone mistily in nameless agonies.
Five sons, and four were dead!
The clock ticked desolation to their ears
And silence gripped the moments as they passed
Too terrible, too passionless for tears.
At last,
Stronger than he, she curbed herself and smiled
And held him weeping like a weary child
Before the first immensity of pain.
Yet once again
She conjured scenes beyond the darkened cloud
That blurred the soul's horizon, as aloud
She spoke his name, and whispered little things
More pregnant than the utterance of kings.

That night she moved,
Spurred by devotion for the man she loved,
Without a pause for sorrow, or a breath
To murmur at the closing walls of death;
Love-steeled and queenly every step she trod;
She climbed unfaltering, serenely browed,
Until she touched the very feet of God
Undaunted and unbowed.
And there in mystic awe
Slow-turning wheels of evolution spun
The poised and pulsing universe. She saw
All life and death synonymous, and birth

The dawn of human wonderment begun
(Birth of all birth) in other realms afar.
Below, ice-pivoted revolved the earth,
A traveller's joy it seemed, a mile-stone star,
Half-glowing, bathed in sun . . .

At dawn they met and found each other's eyes,
Asked the same questions, sought the same replies:
Their last and youngest fought where harsh commands
Still goaded forward lashed and driven bands,
Where Vaux and Thiaumont twin sentinels
Loomed stalwartly. And still a howl of shells
Shattered the Verdun battlements in vain;
Still domineered that keen death-tutored brain
Behind an army deaf to angry scorn,
The boast forgotten and the mask outworn.
At length she spoke: 'Go quickly now,' she said,
'Quick, the next hurrying hour may see him dead.
Find the Great Overlord and tell him all
Quick, for our boy may pass beyond recall
Meanwhile. He shall know happiness to come,
He, the last scion of our stricken home,
Shall blossom like a flower in early Spring,
I say it, I who bore him. Time shall bring
The old primeval happiness to birth
If there be any justice upon earth.'
She ceased; it seemed her voice re-echoed still
As strung with hope he hurried on until
He reached the palace and besought for grace
To see his royal master face to face.

That night in sudden joy he argued away
Across Lorraine, for in his wallet lay
An order blazoned with the royal seals.
Hour after hour the car's revolving wheels

30

Rushed dizzily towards the high command
That held his son in fee. Around, the land
Awoke in changeless Spring. Four steady hours
They travelled, till the bloom of passing flowers
Brought tidings of the dawn. Then to his ears
Rumbled a distant thunder, sudden fears
Urged onward faster. Now the country showed
First signs of war-flung tentacles, the road
Lay pitted here and there, a wounded tree
No longer framed its lordly symmetry.
And soon the land whereon all life was stilled
Became as Man had willed.
At last his journey ended. Long delayed
He sought his goal, now pressing on, now stayed,
Until outside the place of high command
The royal warrant burning in his hand
He knocked – was bidden enter – tense and mute
He faced the marshal with a grave salute
And showed the royal word.
The crowded room was silent, no man stirred –
A pause as long as death, then, dragged and slow,
A voice – 'Your son was killed an hour ago.'
A clock importunately unconcerned
Repeated tick – tick – tick. His eyes discerned
A pen vague-sprawling, madly spiderwise.
Not a man glanced – Yet all the room had eyes:
Not a man spoke – Yet clamorous voices cried:
Stumbling, he walked outside.

A TRENCH INCIDENT

We waited, as the thundering curtain swept
Our sector, and torn shards of iron fell;
Dust from the parapet in showers leapt
   Swirled up by bursting shell.

We waited, like a storm-bespattered ship
That flutters sail to free her grounded keel;
The tingling moments tightened every grip
   On rifles lanced with steel.

We knew the man who led us. All could hear
His ringing voice re-echo loud and strong,
Born of that higher bravery when fear
   Is battled into song.

Then sudden fury lulled and far behind
Like angered beasts our batteries replied –
And suddenly he stumbled, dazed and blind,
   He lay, but ere he died

He struggled for a while, then dimly smiled,
Wrapped in the comradeship of happy things,
Before he entered like a wondering child
   The heritage of kings.

THE FRENCH MOTHER TO HER UNBORN
CHILD

Beat quietly, hid heart.
Build, little limbs; and brain divinely wrought,
Grow, grow in peace. Around, the pangs of war
Are powerless to cripple thee or mar
Thy sure perfection. But, if Death besought
For thee, our tethered souls could never part:
Beat quietly, hid heart.
Form, primal thought,
Close-furled and sheltered as the budding Spring,
Unknown, unknowing, yet divinely planned.
But stay awhile, for sounds of battle ring.
Stir, little hand
Unrealized – I count the dragging hours
And yearn to see it clutch at yonder flowers;
To see thy lucent feet and dimpled frame
And gaze at heav'n-snatched eyes and know thy name,
But stay awhile.
For thou art best alone away from Man:
Wait longer, tears unshed and lurking smile
Of joy enshrined where every joy began.
Time hurries as the moments thump along
(Hark, little ears, my heart is beating strong)
Life is aglow, alive, a perfect song.
Around the land is ugly, but apart
I fashion thee in thought. Now hush, for sleep
Is here. Close, eyes unopened, voice unheard,
Be still. Grow on in beauty till day creep . . .
Hark to my whispered word –
Beat quietly, hid heart.

ENVOI

Below my room, the noise and measured beat
   Of marching men re-echo loud and clear;
Now bobbing cavalry swing down the street,
   Now mules and rumbling batteries draw near.
But all grows dim – the rolling wagon-streams
   To Amiens between the aspen trees,
The stables, billets, men and horses seem
   But murmurs of forgotten fantasies.

Only my dreams are still aglow, a throng
   Of scenes that crowded through a waiting mind,
A myriad scenes. For I have swept along
   To foam ashriek with gulls, and rowed behind
Brown oarsmen swinging to an ocean song,
   Where stately galleons bowed before the wind.

The Somme, 1916

POTPOURRI *or* WHAT YOU WILL

From THE DEATH OF PAN

The river dawdled silver-clean,
  A lane of mirrored sky,
Through marsh and lawn of jewelled green
  And restless fields of rye;
Through haze and heat, and round the feet
  Of meadow-sweet July.

I saw it splash in revelry
  Along a pebbly shallow;
And leap in mimic devilry
  To meet a bowing willow;
I saw it flow benign and slow
  Beneath the gaping swallow.

I knew the choral litany
  Of wind-adoring trees;
Of bramble, rose, and betony,
  And forest symphonies;
The scent of thyme and dewy lime,
  The drone of burglar bees.

Leaf-muffled song and chatter shook
  A bush beside me cheerily;
High over trees a high lark took
  The higher blue unwearily;
Below, square-headed owls awoke
  And ogled downward eerily.

Because, in every blade and bush,
  A shuddering began;
And from behind a flowering rush
  There rose a bearded man
In silence – save a whispered 'Hush!'
  The hush of hornéd Pan;

Among the reeds and water-weeds
  The hush of hornéd Pan.

A lightless mole looked up aware,
  A blind-worm saw and heard,
And everywhere in thrilling air
  No feathered soul or furred
Was heard to rustle anywhere,
  No petal even, stirred;
No bud beneath her silken sheath,
  No flower's breath was heard.

I saw the spiral horns appear
  And eyes of Pan a-peep –
Above the rushes rising clear;
  I saw a squirrel creep
About his neck, beneath his ear
  A baby owl asleep.

I saw his swarthy form and face
  Rise through the ruffled leaves,
All dappled by the living lace
  The wind of shadow weaves;
But in the sun his figure shone
  Gold-brown as burnished sheaves.

Half-god he was (his cloven heels
  And shaggy limbs of speed
Outflew the wind and left behind
  An arrow flying freed)
And half a man. And now he kneels
  To pluck a hollow reed.
He blew the call of calls. He blew,
  And all the spear-like rushes stirred;
He blew the call Narcissus knew
  And Echo overheard.

The call of quiet, and the call,
    The drowsy call of dreams,
The flowing fall and purling call
    Of pebble-broken streams.
Of honey-cells and faint hare-bells
    And flowery charioteers;
The sigh of aspen sentinels,
    The wrath of churning weirs.

He blew the call and over all
Arose a whirl and swirl of wings;
A babble-squabble-bickering,
A squeak and shriek and twittering,
A hustling, bustling, flittering –
From forest roof and forest floor
Came bird and beast with more and more
Strange gifts from every greenwood store,
Of forest cloth the forest weaves,
Fruit, berries, nuts, and dying leaves,
Sky-splashed in baths of dusk and dawn:
Green grasses, mould, and flowery lawn.
From forest roof and forest floor,
There came all creeping, leaping things,
Even the lime and sycamore
Shook off seed-laden wings.

Sunbars through the forest slanting
    Paint a flashing fisher-king,
Now a swaying bough enchanting –
    Now a gleam of blue a-wing –
Larder-laden squirrels panting
    To the brown bark cling.

From the wild of wold and heather
    Rill and hill of rolling blue,

38

Low and high land, marsh and dry land,
  River, field, and forest too;
Fur and feather flock together;
  Ouzel, meadow-mouse, and shrew.

Listen! have you heard a cry,
  Have you heard a sound?
In the growing murmur mingled,
Have you heard a shout that tingled,
  Have you heard a sound,
From the high and leafy sky,
  Or the ground?

O, I heard a noise of laughter,
  Loud the laughter grew:
Grew a noise of joy and laughter
Blown away – now blowing after,
And a boy of joy and laughter
  Nearer, nearer drew:
Near the glade, and every blade
Eye and ear and heart betrayed
A leap of fear, a cheep of fear,
'Who is here? We are afraid.'
Then all the flowers faintly cried –
'Furred and feathered, lithe of limb,
Fly or burrow, leap or swim,
We are tethered, we are tied,
Furred and feathered, flee and hide!'

Nearer, breathlessly he ran
Through the burning corn,
Hair of amber, hue of Pan,
Happy naked child of man;
(Bowing barley o'er him kissing
Shivering barley, quivering, hissing)

Swimming through the brimming corn,
Breathlessly he ran.

Loudly Pan to beast and bird
    Blew the crying call
(Has the field and forest heard,
    Heard the dying call?)
Only lonely breezes blurred
Pool and shadow; never a word
Came from forest, house, or hole,
Squirrel, meadow-mouse, or mole,
    Never, never a word.

Through the barley ripened early
    Flaming apple-cheeks of June,
Hair of honey blowing curly,
    Burnished amber of the moon,
Romped the boy; his figure burly,
    Rolling surely to a tune;
Lithely dancing, leaping, prancing,
    That entrancing afternoon.

Breathlessly, until aweary
    In the gloom-enchanted glade
Dumb and eerie, dumb and dreary,
    Breathlessly he sank afraid.
Who had made the forest eerie?
    Only lonely breezes played
Ruffled terror o'er the mirror
    Of the river round the glade.

How should he know, he a child,
    Yet the foe of Pan,
Conscious beings of the wild
    Dread the name of Man,

Dread and dread, alive or dead,
  Sight and sound of Man?

As a guest who comes unbidden
  Feels the lack of cheer,
As a child in anger chidden
  Feels a lonely fear,
So the boy – for all lay hidden –
  Dumb and lone and drear –
Wandered, wandered, nearly crying,
  Wandered till he found
Pan low-lying, slowly dying,
  On the ferny ground;
Till, appalled, he called and called,
  Wildly called around.

High above the forest roof
  Rustled no reply;
Furred and feathered hung aloof,
  Left their lord to die;
Nor a sound from underground
  Rustled a reply.

Though he called, his arms outreaching,
  Called by name to beast and bird,
Though he called, his voice beseeching,
  'Hurry! hurry!' no one heard,
Echoes only, loud and lonely,
  Not a gesture, not a word.

Silence. So the boy beside him
  Lay and nursed the god alone,
Lovingly he tried to hide him
  From the wind as chill as stone;
Lovingly the boy beside him
  Warmed his body with his own.

41

And the god looks up and wonders
　　At the human kiss,
Dimly wonders, dully ponders,
　　'Who, O, who is this?'
Ere he lies in death, and flies
　　From the chrysalis.

Light and shrivelled, limply drooping,
　　Lies the wizened shell outworn;
And the boy in sorrow stooping,
　　Sees the staring eyes forlorn
Filmy dim; and lifting him,
　　Palely stumbles through the corn.

Nothing hearing, nothing heeding
　　Through the shivering corn and sighing,
Swollen urns of poppies seeding,
　　'Mid the flames of poppies flying,
Blind with tears, his brown knees bleeding,
　　Up the hill he stumbled, crying.

Where the leafless sky is grey
　　There he dug a grave,
There away from shameful day
　　One he could not save
He did lay; and there to-day
　　Spurge and sorrel wave.

New buds never blossom there
　　Ever chill and still,
Snowy flakes of Februeer,
　　Celandine, nor squill,
Mignonette, nor violet.
　　Daisy nor daffodil . . .

'WE POETS OF THE PROUD OLD LINEAGE'

Apart we labour, and alone we climb
The barren heights; for we the singing throng
Whose lives were hallowed by impassioned song
Must die or prove unworthy of our rhyme.
Man after man – we know the price of wars
Who watched the mask of Night whilst others slept,
And spread our laughter far and wide, but kept
Our tears and terror privy to the stars.

O magic gift omnipotent, to sing
And conjure Heaven from surrounding Hell.
Our lips and eyes are touched (for we have seen
Celestial weavers at the loom of Spring).
But O the iron bitterness and keen
Of voices ever clamouring farewell!

THE SHADOW

I stood one night where rivers pause to meet
And mingle in the traffic-rumbling sea:
The surge and clamour of a London street,
In tides alternate, rolled impassively.
Before my feet
Ran shouting boys, and through the pallid glare
Loomed gaunt leviathans that swayed and roared
Past glittering shops, and stations which outpoured
Load after weary load; and everywhere
Strange sounds, a snatch of laughter, shout or word,
Sleek-coated motor-cars that softly purred
Round corners sounding with the rustling beat
Of hurried swarms of feet.
And yet I seemed alone, and dumb-amazed
Before a towering building, wherein blazed
One staring patch of light, one amber square
That shone enshrouded by the dome of night
High in the naked air. And still I gazed
Until a shadow passed across the blind:
A shadow-woman pacing time away
Beside a bed, wherein a poet lay
Dying, dying. One whose mind
(A womb of beauty whereof love was lord)
Had fashioned symphonies of thought and word
Impassionately sweet. And suddenly
She paused – I saw the shadow of her hand
Stretch out and shudder back. I saw her stand
All sorrow-bound in graven dignity.
She bowed her head, her shoulders taut with pain,
Her figure burdened with the weight of tears.
Then all grew dark. And in my waking ears
The traffic surged again.

EVERYCHILD

We take you through Pacific seas
   To islands strange and new,
Where howling monkeys scale the trees
Alive with humming-birds and bees,
Where shiny seals and porpoises
   Snort in the rolling blue.

Then quicker than a shaft of light
   We shear the arctic foam,
And lounging bears of polar white
Roar loudly through the dancing night,
And drive the killer-whales to flight –
   Upon the floor at home.

O hear the chant of Eastern song
   Beneath Arabian stars,
Where camels slowly stalk along
And gleaming Arabs, tall and strong,
Buy gold and merchandise among
   The riot of bazaars!

The glow-worms crawl excitedly
   And trim their lamps o' night;
For often, ere the moon is high,
Bat-harnessed walnut-shells flit by
To bear them to the waiting sky
   And set the stars alight.

The nodding poplars understand
   And birds and beasts and flowers:
And we shall wander hand in hand
With better things than Peter Panned –
O what is footlight fairyland
   Beside this world of ours?

What matter if the clouds are grey
  Or winter-keen and wild,
When you and I have found a way
To turn November into May;
For Everyjoy is Everyday
  And Everyman a child.

CHILD OF THE FLOWING TIDE

Away to the call of the racing sea –
  (Child of the flowing tide)
A hundred chargers of ivory,
And two of them saddled for you and for me,
Are pawing and stamping the surf to be free
  Where the wild sea-horses ride.
The deep water shall roar as we race from the shore
  On the back of the flowing tide.

O hurry, the moon is away in the sky
  (Child of the flowing tide)
With your heels well down, and your heart set high
You're saddled and bridled, and so am I;
So gather your reins, for the foam will fly
  Where the wild sea-horses ride.
Grip tight with your knees as you gallop the seas
  On the back of the flowing tide.

On the wide lagoon I'll meet you to-night
  (Child of the flowing tide)
When the moon swings high and the stars are alight
And the roaring sea-chargers are ready to fight:
Their manes are all foam and their coats are all white
  Where the wild sea-horses ride.
The deep waters shall roar as we race from the shore
  On the back of the flowing tide.

EIGHT SONNETS

I

I tremble at the outset, for I know
How rhythm halts and rhyme rings falsely true.
Yet courage, your disciple, bids me show
That speech may offer sacrifice to you.
Vain boast! For if success in splendour came
Poised faultlessly in lines of perfect stress,
I must fall short of it in very shame
Unworthy of my sonnet's worthiness.

But should I fail, and feel the words I sought
Elusive, or bedecked with frail disguise
Of tattered sentiment, that risk I dare
Not hazard in the winding maze of thought,
Lest I should stir the wonder in your eyes
Or wind a little tangle in your hair.

II

So let me fail: what matter if the wise
And worldly whisper, who so poor as they?
For everywhere alike the common way
Has now become an earthly paradise.
And where you walk the very pavement cries
Of blue-bells, April-chimed, and fawns at play;
And London seems a sylvan holiday
Of flower-hunting bees and butterflies.

So let me fail, for where I could succeed
How mean the quest, a climber gazing down
From the low vantage of some petty hill.
But chance success would be the gambler's thrill

48

Who plays with God for worlds, and wins indeed
The whole of Paradise for half-a-crown!

III

I have no room for jealous gods, and find
No ring of joy or laughter in the Creed,
Nor shall my great possession be resigned
In fear or favour of my spirit's need.
For joy is mine, and mine the teeming years
Unfettered in a world impassionate;
Not mine a sorrowed Calvary of tears
Where love was vassal to the lords of hate.

Let others bow before a God unknown
Enshrined in words they dimly understand.
Let every man make Paradise his own –
My Goddess breathes and leads me by the hand
O hush! I dare not speak of it alone,
'Tis all too wonderful and strangely planned!

IV

Day after day my growing pinions beat
Impatiently. Yet, in a place unclean
I sought the dwarfed, the petty and obscene,
And aped the clownish mummers of the street;
Till suddenly the world grew strangely sweet,
All eager at a touch, and thrilling-keen;
With half-forgotten hands I strove unseen
To mould a little planet at your feet.

You spoke and there was light, and slowly grew
My teeming world of verse, a brotherhood

Of music, thought, and wonder, born anew,
Alive, aglow, in every varied mood.
And when the waking truth is bursting through
I feel you bend to see that all is good.

V

If I had seen what hourly happiness
In this my world your being could ordain,
How then should I have trysted with distress
And misery the cringing friend of pain?
If I had seen beyond the looming years
Your shadow, grief had haunted me in vain,
For what are cataracts of human tears
Beside the boundless laughter of the main?

O barren days bygone! Now every field
Wakes clamorous with dawning life conceived,
So has the magic universe revealed
Whole happiness to one who half believed –
Whole happiness, and in my heart concealed
Wide wonder at the sacrament received.

VI

'Great men and happy years,' you say from these
Your knowledge came, and your diviner powers
More thrilling than the honey-womb of flowers
Or the bright star-foam of the Pleiades.
So, did you learn the droning lore of bees
From some be-medalled soldier? Did you meet
Madonna-hearted statesmen in the street,
Or bishops, babbling of the opal seas?

O poor deceiver, conscript joys belong
To you as homage. For the happy years
Bear fruit to-day, and blossom like the flowers
That breathe of summertime in after hours.
For you were loyal to a creed of Song
Nor ever stooped to misery and tears.

VII

Would I could throw my stuttering self away
And shrine the soul wherein all wonders beat,
Would I were you, for one brief holiday
The whole shy universe before my feet.
O happiness, to know joy's secret mine,
To hold adoring ministers in fee,
Narcissus-like to bless the Serpentine
And with the stars outdance Terpsichore.

For once a poet sang of happiness,
But now, like running flame, glad voices say –
'Joy is the sheer antithesis of wrong.'
Enough, – and I, no longer comradeless,
Behold exultant on the world's highway
Your being, and the proof of Pippa's song.

VIII

When you are old and dancing shadows play
Around the sky-blown laughter in your eyes
Shall I, unworthy of your new disguise,
Forget the sacrament and go away?
Shall I adore, like sorrowed men to-day,
The child who gurgled in first ecstasies

51

At oxen (Mary said) that mooed surprise
And snuffed with wondering muzzles in the hay?

O leave the past – the living world is mine
Warm, passionate, and breathing. Even so
Shall Life in after years make Earth divine
And fire shall burn as long as embers glow.
But he who babbled to the wondering kine
Is dead, long dead, two thousand years ago.

KEATS

Touch me, O Lord, and let my sonnet ring
With echoes. Now his words of crowned belief
In raging hours of pain and suffering
Too high for praise, too terrible for grief,
Ring loud and clear. Last night his chariot rolled
And I beheld him urge amid the stars
Cloud-fashioned steeds of snow moon-aureoled,
Himself a charioteer equipped for wars.

Faster and faster – men of Blood and Pain
Opposed in vast battalions, but he
Rolled back their army to the dark again
And triumphed while he sang exultingly
As now he sings. Boy of the glowing brain,
Dear Keats your name is Paradise to me!

REACTION

Afraid, afraid, I sought the kindly night
In fear that mocking fools should scrutinise
The beauty I discovered in men's eyes,
And mock me as a dreaming anchorite.
For long in fear I sinned against the light
And shrouded Poetry with vain disguise;
Before I sang, unconscious as the skies,
Self-chanting songs to me supreme delight.

But now, O littlest of all little minds,
High-browed, alone, aloof, you little know
How like you are to Brown, who lifts the blinds
Of his suburban villa, just to show
That he alone is up, but always finds
The neighbourhood awoke an hour ago!

THE STROLLING SINGER

Sun-bathed in Summer peace the village lay
That afternoon. Along the happy street
Milk-fragrant kine, and wagons high with hay
Came lumbering. The fields were loud with bees
And drowsy with the wind-stirred meadowsweet.
From bowing trees
Fell chatter, and above the garden wall
Wide sunflowers beamed at spearing hollyhocks
That dared the wind, and scorned the clustered stocks,
And bore their laddered blooms high over all.

Here amid Summer murmur and delight
The strolling singer came. The people heard
Stray snatches of a song – a laugh – a word,
And gossiping in groups of two or three
Stood all amazed. For no one came in sight,
Only the wind was laden drowsily
With mellow sounds that slowly growing strong
At last became a song:

    'Bend down, the marsh and meadow holds
       Pale yellow pimpernels,
    And sun-begotten marigolds,
       Thyme, orchis, asphodels,
    And borage born of ocean blue,
    Plumed armoured thistles, fever-few,
    Sea-campion globed, and clinging dew
       In giant flower-bells.

    'Bend down – an ebon beetle prowls,
       And there a swinging bee
    Drinks honey from the laden cowls
       That clothe the foxglove tree.

And giant peacock butterflies
Light meadowsweet with sudden eyes,
And through the tangled grasses rise
   Lucerne and timothy.'

Louder and louder grew the voice, until
A figure specked the heaven-touching hill,
And nearer, nearer, still . . .
The villagers in mingled fear and awe
Stood round on tiptoe waiting. Soon they saw
A little sylvan man with beckoning eyes
And limbs of lithe expression. Woven flowers
And grasses, splashed with rainbow-tinted showers,
And jewelled with alluring butterflies,
Enwrapped him. Russet face, clear-featured, gay
As pebble-rumpled streams, and tousled hair
Sun-dyed and naked. His limbs were bronzed and bare,
And sprang, it seemed, from the wild interplay
Of flower-woven garb. Around his waist
Twined traveller's-joy and honeysuckle, sweet
And freshly dewed, and on his lissom feet
Were pointed shoes of silver beech rush-laced.

The village gazed in silence, till a child
Began: 'Who are you, funny man?
Your face seems to be telling truth, your eyes
Are just the colour of blue butterflies,
O tell us who you are?'
The stranger smiled,
And turned his face that bore the wistful, far,
Strange wonder-look of one whose dreams come true,
Who delves in darkened quarries of his brain
Unhoped-for gold, and changes old to new
As Spring rejuvenates the earth again.
Of one who plays Narcissus in Life's pool

And sees an image strangely beautiful . . .
Then suddenly they heard him cry:

> 'Come buy,
> I own the laughing earth.
> And all my chanted words are deeds;
> I follow where my fancy leads,
> And sell my songs for mirth.
> What will you buy?

> 'Speak hurriedly, and choose your song,
> The poplar's shadow creeps along,
> Search hurriedly the Earth and Sky,
> What will you buy?'

Meanwhile a crowd had gathered, in a ring;
The butcher, grocer, postman, parson, clerk,
And all the village, open-mouthed and stark,
Stood mutely marvelling;
And children clamoured round him with large eyes
And pelted him for songs, like countless hail,
With pleadings, shouts and cries:

> 'Sing us a song of Paradise,
> Of railway engines, fawns,
> Of stolen queens in guarded towers,
> Of sprites and leprechauns' –
> O HUSH! All were dumb –
> 'Boy in blue smock, sucking your thumb,
> With hair like a tangled chrysanthemum,
> What would you like me to sing, Oceaneyed?'

Loud the boy's answer rang,
> '*I* want a song of flowers!'
And this is the song he sang:

> 'Sisters of mercy are Cyclamen,

57

Snowdrops and Arums too,
But Primulus, Violets, Stocks, Mignonette,
Crocus aflame, and the Never Forget,
Are chaster than chastity too.
Now sulphur Laburnum and Lilac, adieu,
Good-bye April children to you!
For who
Will climb up the flowers of my Hollyhock towers
With butterfly steeple-jacks blue?
But, climber, beware!
Of Love-in-a-mist in a tangle of hair,
Of thistly Teazles, and wingèd Sweet-Peas
With tentacle tendrils that strangle with ease,
Of butterfly Orchis a–clamour for bees.
For Dragon may Snap you, and Sundew may trap you,
Before you have started, before you have parted
The grass at the foot of my Hollyhock trees.
But think of the view
Of the whole garden side!
   We'll charter a dragon–fly homeward, and ride
   Down to our Rosemary, Marjoram, Rue,
   Lavender, London Pride.'

All watched him, held, bewitched, and with him clung
To the green tops of slowly swaying towers,
Where bees had scattered pollen-dust, that hung
Above the teeming nectaries of flowers,
And all again were young.
But now the poplars cast their phantom bars
In latticed shadows; now a scarf unfurled,
Like parrot-tulip petals hued and torn,
Across the West was flung.

And now, before the twilight bares the stars,
Ere jewelled night is born,

All silently the Singer left the world.
Beyond the hill he passed,
But singing all the while; first loud and strong,
Then fainter, till at last
Came only jumbled echoes of a song:

> 'Bend down – the marsh and meadow holds
>   Pale yellow Pimpernels,
> And sun-begotten Marigolds
>   Thyme, Orchis, Asphodels' . . .
> (Fainter and fainter it grew
> Gentle as ebbing tide)
> 'Butterfly steeple-jacks blue' . . .
> (Fainter it grew
> And died)
> Echoing 'Rosemary, Marjoram, Rue,
>   Lavender, London Pride.'

AMBITION

If ever in some anthology of fame
A thought of mine is treasured, may my name
Be not appended like a label tied
To some poor plant at last identified.
Whether the thought be one of rarest worth,
A glimpse of Earth in Heaven or Heaven on Earth;
Or register some flower's unique delight
And make it more real in the reader's sight;
Or strike the reader in the heart and head
As truth that he himself has felt and said.
For sleeping thoughts give birth to poets' cries
As chrysalis give birth to butterflies;
But did God create butterflies for credit?
He wrote the poem, did he care who read it
When, in the boyhood of ingenuous Time,
The Brontosaurus in primordial slime
Wallowed? But though that monster may have been
No thing of beauty but a thing obscene,
Did he not cry with joy: 'It moves – it moves!'
And, like the poet at the words he loves,
Work on and on till man, the best beast, stood,
Made in his image, better if not yet good?
For what are Truth and Goodness in his sight? –
Sufficient for the day the day's delight.

A BLESSING

May your garden count the hours
With her wild and garden flowers;
May cold crocus candles glow;
Poised and hanging drops of snow;
Primulas and daffodils;
Nodding harebells from the hills;
Closed and tattered tulips creaking
Stalk to stalk, mimosa seeking
Spots to catch the bee uncaring
With first honey homeward faring;
And first green your garden stay
From rise of March to fall of May.

When your Spring to Summer grows
May the puffed and rampant rose
Mingle hers with scent of stocks;
May sweet-peas in fluttering flocks,
More your heart than twigs entwine;
May the dancing columbine
In her frock of frailest blue
Hold your heart entangled too.
Ramblers round you twine and twist;
Love in all his maze of mist;
May Miss Perkins bloom elately,
Evening primroses sedately;
Lilies of the valley chime
And tell the time below the lime.

When rich Autumn fills your figs
And breathes bloom on your grapes; may grigs
Hop in the heavy grass when pops
The glowing gorse; may mushroom tops
With gills of pink and domes of cream

Amid your dewy meadows gleam.
And when winged dragons, bronze and blue,
With oozy hidden haunts in view,
Vie with the last bees booming by –
When late birds ride the racing sky –
May your fasting garden sing
The coming festival of Spring.

FAREWELL TO ROMANY

Goodbye, dear friend. If we no more shall roam
   Fresh woods with you, nor fields your voice made cool;
Nor find the fieldmouse in his harvest home,
      The brown trout in the pool.

Nor with hands made more gentle at your words,
   Pick up the shrew mouse or the trembling hare;
Nor, with ears wiser, name the singing birds
      In trees no longer bare.

If we no more with you shall do these things,
   Let us, at least, say sometimes when the clear
Spring skies are full of song and woods with wings,
      'I wish that he was here.'

Then shall we keep your memory green and true;
   Then shall the lovely world more lovely grow,
And you, dear Romany, I think that you
      Would wish to have it so.

DEAR LOVE THE PAST

Dear love the past is flowing round the present.
　　The barriers fall and eased now is the stress
　　Of feuds wherein we strove but failed to squander
　　The rich investment of our happiness.
　　The marbled sands their old, ribbed strength recover
　　Careless no more but carefree let us wander.

We have no need to delve in dusty pages
　　To evoke the dead past from long quiet sifted
　　Fragments which down the stream of time have drifted,
　　What is to us the rancour of past ages,
　　Now hand in hand again, our hearts uplifted.

Dear love, those axes we should not have wielded
　　Were blunted on the roots that bind us ever,
　　How could we think that we with steel could sever
　　The branches of our tree stout-timber-hearted?
　　Those hidden roots deep underground, unparted,
　　How could we ever dream they would have yielded?

COME, LET'S NOT BRIEF . . .

Come, let's not brief ourselves to accuse the other
Or marshal facts to give the lie to each.
The Judge won't hear our case, why should He bother?
His Word he reckons worth more than our speech.
Why do we sigh for the past and think it the fairest
Or let the past the present prepossess?
Why do we ask so much more now, my dearest,
When once we were content with so much less?

O love, my love, time shall your body wither,
But you have put like Browning in your breast
Power of your spirit's youth, an eagle's feather,
Golden in service and in friendship blessed,
Come, let us start freshly again together,
And let's remember to forget the rest.

UNSEEN

There was no sign, the landscape solid stood
And blown clouds frothed the sun's fall through a bath
Of claret merged with orange, yet the wood,
The stream, and every hillock, hedge, and path

I knew was full of life . . . an adder crept
And flickered like his own worm-flickering tongue;
The dewfall owl in darkening shadow slept;
Over the hill the swallows southward swung.

The boy-faced baby otters were at play;
The kingfisher had hidden his blaze of blue;
Hunching his back a weasel went his way;
I knew the wren was sleeping, and I knew

A bat unfurled his weft-winged sails and sped;
A harvest-mouse swarmed up an ear of corn;
A snouted shrew-mouse in an owl's beak bled;
A bird was killed, another bird was born.

Without a sign or sound these things were done,
Beneath the sunset whilst I waited there;
But had I seen them starkly in the sun,
The sight could not have made me more aware.

BON VOYAGE

Children on Holiday by the Sea

And what are gay as sparkling eyes
    The hand above them shades?
What cooler than foam-marbled sands
    Or, tide-revealed, the glades
Which from his lair of dappled hues
    The hueless prawn invades?

Long may you peer deep into pools
    And wonder on your knees;
And sink, perchance, some bits of shell
    In plumed anemones
That stain the light-deflected aisles
    And altars of the seas.

So much and more we pray for you
    The tides may bring and bless
Somewhere around these precious Isles
    Our careless seas caress
A heritage of play for you
    In haunts of happiness.

SONG FROM THE SELSEA PAGEANT, 1965

(A medieval milkmaid, a mother, Emma, Queen
of King Canute, who with her ladies made
vestments in cloth of gold and silver.)

They sing

Churn, churn the milk in the drum
As in kingdom past so in kingdom come.
Honour these hands that mended and made,
Hands that the will of God obeyed,
That made and mended not maimed and marred
The gold wheat garnered, the honey jarred.

Rock, rock the cradle in faith,
A boy is born in defiance of death,
Serf or slave no lord is he
(Mother of God no lady she)
The woman will glean where the corn was sown,
And the grass grow green on her grave unknown.

Weave, weave the song unsung
Of the hands of a queen long dead when young,
Cloth she wove of a golden sheen
(Quietly working sits the Queen)
May her fingers speak in golden thread
Of peace triumphant when war is dead.

OTHER CREATURES SEEN
LIGHTHEARTEDLY

THE BRONTOSAURUS

'The First Dawn broke,' the lecturer began,
'When Homer gave the written word to Man.
God was made manifest, and yet, we know
That Homer lived three thousand years ago!'
The old professor paused. A sunbeam caught
A skeleton behind him. This we thought
Rather unfortunate. For there before us
The breast bones of a ponderous Brontosaurus
Gleamed suddenly, and, as the sun lit upon
The mighty Mesozoic skeleton,
The beast seemed living and dragging through the heat
Of steaming swamp his length of fifty feet,
Huge tail, small head high perched, enormous neck,
Curved like an ostrich just about to peck:
O, would he move those huddled legs and wave
That tail and sweep the lecturer to his grave?
Snort through that single nostril as we know
He snorted just ten million years ago?

BLUE WHALE

I can assure you this is true,
The Whale when born (I mean the Blue)
Weighs eight *tons*! Yes, it makes you think,
And so rich is the milk they drink
They put on – every mother's son –
Each day a quarter of a ton.

So if unwieldy is your girth
Do not unduly this deplore,
You didn't weigh eight tons at birth –
That's something to be grateful for.

O wouldn't you like to be a whale
   And sail serenely by,
An eighty-foot whale from your tip to your tail
   And a tiny, briny eye?
Wouldn't you like to wallow
   Where nobody says 'Come out!'
Wouldn't you like to swallow
   And blow all the brine about?
Wouldn't you like to be always clean
But never to have to wash, I mean,
   And wouldn't you love to spout
   O yes, just think –
   A feather of spray as you sail away
   And rise and sink and rise and sink
     And blow all the brine about?

This piece, set to music, was performed
all over the world by Hoagy Carmichael

BIRDS

Eagles, you browless birds, who skim
The sky on poised and feathered limb,
You whom no sky's top terrifies,
Taught me the terror of the skies.

Cold cormorants, your spray-wet sheen,
Your cold bead eyes of glassy green,
And bubbling death-dive, swift and steep,
Taught me the terror of the deep.

Red-eyed, red-clawed, you vultures keen
Who find no carrion flesh unclean,
Who gather and cry at life's last breath,
Taught me the sanctity of death.

You whistling swans, your flapping flight,
A huge-formed arrowhead of white
Over and down the horizon's dip,
Taught me the law of leadership.

You downy-eiders, from your breasts
Plucking the down to build your nests,
Taught me, as no commandment could,
The sacrifice of motherhood.

THE SNAKE

Lipless, lidless, sinuous thing
What need have you of leg or wing?

Oarless bark your body grips
The roughened earth and forward slips,
Slithering behind the thread
Of a flickering tongue in a flattened head.
Smoothly-skinned and warmly dry
In one-piece-moving symmetry,
Snake whose crush is no caress,
Snake whose strike is pitiless,
Who could rise to your disdain
Or such integrity contain?

Unrepentant, lovely brute you,
Let them curse you, I salute you.

THE GIRAFFE

Hide of a leopard and hide of a deer
   And eyes of a baby calf,
Sombre and large and crystal clear,
And a comical back that is almost sheer
   Has the absurd giraffe.

A crane all covered with hide and hair
   Is the aslant giraffe,
So cleverly mottled with many a square
That even the Jungle is unaware
Whether a pair or a herd are there,
   Or possibly one giraffe,
   Or possibly only half.

If you saw him stoop and straddle and drink
   He would certainly make you laugh,
He would certainly make you laugh, I think,
With his head right down on the water's brink,
   Would the invert giraffe,
The comical, knock-kneed, angular, crock-kneed,
   Anyhow-built giraffe.

There's more than a grain of common sense
   And a husky lot of chaff
In the many and various arguments
   About the first giraffe,
   The first and worst giraffe:
Whether he grew a neck because
   He yearned for the higher shoots
   Out of the reach of all and each
   Of the ruminating brutes;
Or whether he got to the shoots because
His neck was long, if long it was,

Is the cause of many disputes
Over the ladder without any rungs,
The stopper-like mouth and the longest of tongues
    Of the rum and dumb giraffe,
The how-did-you-come giraffe,
The brown equatorial, semi-arboreal
    Head-in-the-air giraffe.

THE DUCK-BILLED PLATYPUS

Ornithorhyncus anatinus

The Ornithorhyncus
May possibly link us
  Men with oviparous things
Who move on their stomachs instead of on legs
And share the great secret of how to lay eggs
  With creatures that go in for wings.
      The probable link
      Biologists think
  Is the fact (I'm not telling a tale)
That the ornithorhyncus is also a mammal
Like the ant-eater, you, me, or the camel,
    The wallaby, weasel and whale.
  Biologists think of this wonderful creature
  And ask themselves – What sort of soul
Can the Dame Nature, that blunderful teacher,
  Have given the duck and the mole?
For the duck and the mole in the ornithorhyncus
    Are not too unfairly divided,
  But whether such ancestors raise us or sink us,
  And whether the Lords of Eternity think us
  Fit to be heirs of the ornithorhyncus
    Biologists haven't decided.

CONCLUSIONS

HANDS

Now rest in abeyance
    From market and mill
Millions of hands
    Unaware of their skill;
Hands pale as faience,
    Hands brown as hazel,
How can I praise all
    Those that are gifted?
Hands like the rose
    To the wild rose grafted,
How from such good
    Can I choose?
Some lovely food
    Have spicily garnished
(Sauces and stews);
    Others, nail varnished,
Have tapped like the yaffle
    A texture of news.

Now sleep-arrested
    They lie on the pillow,
Or clasped in a fellow,
    Or open, uncurled;
And some are as shell-pink
    As the silk petals
Of roses unfurled,
The soft hands of children,
    The hope of the world.

A PRAYER, II

Lord, when I stand in Thy celestial court
And render thee a poet's last report;
From my worn, working body, dearly prized,
Discharged, or, at the best, demobilised;
Curse me if so thou must, thou art divine,
And say that little verse is worse than mine;
Blue-pencil all, but give me not, I pray,
Upon that (O, I hope long-distant) day
My poems back complete, corrected, clean –
Lord, show me not how good they should have been!

A PILGRIM'S SONG

And didst thou travel light, dear Lord,
   was thine so smooth a road
That thou upon thy shoulders broad
   could hoist our heavy load?
Too frail each other's woes to bear
   without thy help are we;
Can we each other's burdens share
   if we not burden thee?

O wonder of the world withstood!
   That night of prayer and doom
Was not the sunset red with blood,
   the dawn pale as a tomb?
In agony and bloody sweat,
   in tears of love undried,
O undespairing Lord, and yet
   with Man identified.

As in dark drops the pitting rain
   falls on a dusty street,
So tears shall fall and fall again
   to wash thy wounded feet.
But thy quick hands to heal are strong,
   O love, thy patients we,
Who sing with joy the pilgrims' song
   and walk, dear Lord, with thee.

ACKNOWLEDGEMENTS

The compiler's thanks are due to all who have collaborated so readily in effecting publication of this book. I prayed heartily for the uniquely prestigious John Murray imprint; and, lo, my prayer has been answered, for Murray's have produced and published the book without profit to themselves. With matching generosity, Lloyds Bank have looked after receipt and administration of funds most assiduously, not only remitting any charge but positively adding interest at the highest rate.

Those book-world luminaries, Michael Turner and David Whitaker, have provided immense support and encouragement throughout, without fee or reward of any kind, combining the roles of trustees, referees and advisers. Piling Pelion on Ossa, they have also contributed liberally to the fund, while David Whitaker, at a crucial stage, guaranteed the balance then yet to come.

A spontaneous message of warm encouragement from the Archbishop of Canterbury was most heartening at a difficult time, while Field-Marshal Lord Bramall entered the lists at once with a substantial financial contribution and the assurance of continuing support in ways that will be manifest in the event.

Sir David Orr, Sir Peter Walters, Sir Peter Saunders (with Katie Boyle); Book Club Associates and the Mercers are other substantial donors at the time of writing, while the Royal Fusiliers and the Royal Corps of Transport have tipped in with spontaneous generosity, the more marked when one considers the demands upon their stretched resources.

Special tribute is paid in the Introduction, to the amaz-